# 6TH GRADE AMERICAN HISTORY FOUNDING FATHERS AND LEADERS

The founding fathers were those political leaders who were part of the American Revolution against the authority of the British Crown and established the United States of America.

# GEORGE WASHINGTON

was the first President
of the United States.
He presided over the
convention that drafted
the current United States
Constitution and during
his lifetime was called
the father of his country.

# JOHN ADAMS

was the second President
of the United States. As
a Founding Father he
was a principal leader of
American independence
from Great Britain.

# THOMAS JEFFERSON

was the third President
of the United States.
He was the principal
author of the Declaration
of Independence.

# JAMES MADISON

was the fourth President of the United States. He was known as the Father of the Constitution for being instrumental in the drafting of the U.S. Constitution.

# ALEXANDER HAMILTON

was the chief staff aide
to General George
Washington. Hamilton was
made the first Secretary
of the Treasury.

# JAMES MONROE

was the fifth President of
the United States. Monroe
was the last president who
was a Founding Father
of the United States.

# BENJAMIN FRANKLIN

was considered the elder statesman by the time of the Revolution and later Constitutional Convention. He was a member of the Committee of Five that drafted the Declaration of Independence.

# JOHN HANCOCK

served as president of
the Second Continental
Congress. Before the
American Revolution,
Hancock was one of
the wealthiest men in
the Thirteen Colonies.

# JAMES WILSON

was elected twice to the Continental Congress. He emerged as a political leader after the American Revolutionary War.

# JOHN JAY

was the first Chief Justice of
the United States and signer
of the Treaty of Paris. Jay
served as the President of
the Continental Congress,
from 1778 to 1779.

# GOUVERNEUR MORRIS

was a Founding Father
of the United States who
represented Pennsylvania
in the Constitutional
Convention of 1787.
He signed the Articles
of Confederation.

# SAMUEL ADAMS

was a leader of the movement that became the American Revolution. He was a delegate to both the First and Second Continental Congresses and fought for the Declaration of Independence.

# PATRICK HENRY

served as the first and sixth post-colonial Governor of Virginia, from 1776 to 1779 and 1784 to 1786. He also helped fight for the addition of the Bill of Rights to the US Constitution.

# ROBERT MORRIS

financed the American Revolution and signed the Declaration of Independence, the Articles of Confederation, and the United States Constitution.

www.ingramcontent.com/pod-product-compliance
Lightning Source LLC
Chambersburg PA
CBHW081243130726
47997CB00009B/2983